bird book

*A*lso by Laura Walker

rimertown/ an atlas
swarm lure

bird book

laura Walker

shearsman books

2011

First published in the United Kingdom in 2011 by
Shearsman Books Ltd
58 Velwell Road
Exeter EX4 4LD

www.shearsman.com

ISBN 978-1-84861-153-5
First Edition

for Ben and Theo

in poor light   to resemble

      she stood with her back to the lamp

by second winter

a habit of twitching

overgrown field

blue grosbeak

in late summer he becomes

lining

primary and secondary   faint

to call a horse   burr

he would wander and wander

                                        scarlet tanager

obscuring as pastime

a combination of her

       unstreaked and aggressive

      she paused by the back steps

   abundant

house sparrow

yellow spectacle

a suggested house

white-eyed vireo

she awaits a violent body

our more abundant

the larger   a small

       ask him to come in

       mourning dove

night snare

herself wide

four dusky bars

what we lack

what we find

a hollow booming

whose wooded town

jars

branching roof

common nighthawk

he brought it from far away   *spent entirely too much*

to resemble a fish in youth

the curse of commons

we will ourselves calm

roadside

american crow

half of numerous

we were dark   prominent

      two boys in the backseat

    large white peaches

                  to call

                  rapid

                  an only tree

            cavity

     sluggish or stagnant

or water

                    prothonotary warbler

a watery range

fainter or absent

commotion near the woods

northern parula

to differ from one's body

brown creeper

held from above

timed commotion

    stories all in yellow

        what it means *to disguise*

she held her hand to the bed

wilson's warbler

long primary projection

across her upper
white belly lower

to *claim before you go*

flush

flicker

acadian flycatcher

he did not smoke

tendency to soar

chimney

chimney swift

chisel   rival

the bright red of *bargain*

                                   conspicuous

         summer

             harsher and sharper

        door

                              red-headed woodpecker

called something else

    unspent

                    we gather together

      summer nets

           she brought winter

           particular sap

                cedar waxwing

lack what is prominent

she has your eyes

willow flycatcher

become yellow in glass

> *she would not winter*
> *boxes of field peas*

witch

common yellowthroat

grow duller from wear

fences

fluttering thin

again the land she waited

say's phoebe

thinned

        hers the brazen

reduce or absent

      she was broader

      a pale

to take the songbird out of your mouth

      singly

    in the maritime

cooper's hawk

contrasting edge

to become the rare one

great crested flycatcher

her fingers   not thin

exuberant ground

house wren

we saw him walking down from the store

coal headed

to be seldom visible

give in a series

                       stutter

near water

eastern kingbird

to set off in the dark

lacking water   a scarf for the head

thin edge of walking

                              i will not with you

          vary   speech

                         pine warbler

yellow spectacles

tongue a series

she arrived her dress

vagrant

kentucky warbler

slate colored

between some

rapid song

junco

upslur

stem

i move out where you can see me

wood duck

of many habits

a streaked face

we practice piano by dim light

thrush

flaring
        behind   blue

pear at a distance

      he never touched her

    as large as

common

northern goshawk

overall   a forgotten   shade

dead of

things more rapid as it comes

orchard oriole

she rode them in the mornings

something leaping from the meadows

teakettle   *teakettle*

carolina wren

fresh fall

washed yellow

         a habit of pumping

preceding pages

to take the first syllable

farmland

and make something of it

eastern phoebe

overall a forgotten shade

accidental field

sky lark

.

you who resemble

her

        clearings   *borders*

rare to   rare

indigo bunting

the signal   joy

rounded cut above the bone

           they were there again this spring

  abrupt

bluebird

her towering crayon

liquid

this twentieth century

northern cardinal

she came from the east

dark   slatted

    him booming in the night

common nighthawk

large

        dark

prominent

        without bars

                the bells we depend upon

stagnant water

prothonotary warbler

a small night jar

        though poor

up and again

brush on the side road

common poorwill

dress in plain black
to turn her head

in her   less extensive

eastern

we walked among water

downslope

and slur

forage

creeping methodically along the branches

yellow-throated warbler

45

unmusical

hovering

she met him at the edge of the field

dense thicket

yellow-breasted chat

he walked through pines

resembles   lore

acquittal

i won't   beneath her

thin

american redstart

to ask at the porchlight door

her hand among the beans

peter peter peter

inure

tufted titmouse

he was louder   *fleshy*

to resemble her

winter

a series

painted redstart

distinguish blue

                           the child looks like

second winter

poor light

   risen   *fall*

blue grosbeak

seldom visible

wash

hush

and conspicuous

eastern kingbird

ring the likely song

long primary projection

to fall from the bone of

scrape

to accent the first syllable

          he headed northeast

acadian flycatcher

she wore a red cap

to acquire

    he learned to dance here in the house

strident wheat abundant

numerous   sound

house finch

to be seen

        troubled   flash

                white lime of other days

and borrowed

their omitting   sectional cavities

repeat

to be heard at night   its own a kind of harsh

               i do not want you here

   come into my town

northern mockingbird

covets white

        she lacks and covers

marked on the forehead

        we ate standing

to call when you move

        alone in the kitchen

a jar full of weeds

american goldfinch

to labor   year round

unusual in his head

and not like here

      secondary   slip

summer tanager

fairer or absent

trouble rising   these eastern words

especially near water

northern parula

smallest lid

bright   pool

to become transparent with song

second syllable

flint

i won't pretend the colors

least flycatcher

black in good light

to roam blue

                    bottles she lined on the shelves

to learn the german

casual

common grackle

he followed her through the store

darkest head

told from

and out into the street

    compare the lack of

    syllable

        leaves and rafters

eastern phoebe

back

faint dark

    i call you

    unwary

family orchard

downy woodpecker

the yellow of

body

lack

lower branches

prairie warbler

regularly seen

the trail forked

      to be young

      to resemble

she held the screen door

                      ruby-throated hummingbird

casual to very rare

pull you by the sleeve

pine warbler

she was very faintly *his own*

    smaller   darker

   thin mending   across

        she would again dive down

it was a shack

      northeast

loggerhead shrike

pineland

dark with red eyes

drink your tea

eastern towhee

to begin at the top of the head

eyes in   mulled

so fall

dull

it was an accidental meeting

pacific-slope flycatcher

less green

saw him difficult

                            clear variable

   rote

western wood-pewee

corresponding tenses

the light still on

far barn

barn swallow

to lack something prominent

she was just your size

single trajectory

to till the dull ground

migrant   speech

willow flycatcher

throat to breast

weep

the canopy close over

great crested flycatcher

her face

black stride

trees whispering trees

black-throated green warbler

two occur   yellow

in the east   in the north

            embroidered bib

she sewed him in patches

lacking the feminine traits

northern flicker

white cheek

    dig a small hole   burying

    entirely too small

granary   tree

acorn woodpecker

teakettle tea

vary

    to sing for light

    wet and traveling maps

         to return   a harsher light

we grow darker as we travel

wren

descant of rust   variable

gray crowns

a low yank

repeated

this leafy east

white-breasted nuthatch

to dwell in open field

rusty blackbird

to be divided into quadrants

winter

and left there

red-breasted sapsucker

in their own family

to lose your hold

bobwhite

NOTE ON THE TEXT

bird book was written in concert with *Field Guide to the Birds of North America*, third edition, published by National Geographic.

ACKNOWLEDGEMENTS

Many thanks to Albion Books, which published a selection
of these poems as a chapbook, also called *bird book*.
Thanks also to *Thermos* and *Switchback*, where some of
these poems first appeared.

Writing this book would not have been possible without the
community of poets I work among. Many, many thanks to
Brian Teare, Sharon Osmond and her bird-filled garden, and
Ed Smallfield and Valerie Coulton. Ongoing gratitude to the
Joost poets and the Evelyn Street reading group: Susanne
Dyckman, Todd Melicker, Steve Hemenway, Megan Pruiett,
Monica Regan, Tiff Dresser, Doug MacPherson, and
Sharon Osmond. Much gratitude also to Tony Frazer and
Jaime Robles, for turning these pages into a book. And, as
always, many thanks to my family, who inspired me to
write in small spaces.